Original title:
Sap and Soil

Copyright © 2025 Creative Arts Management OÜ
All rights reserved.

Author: Giselle Montgomery
ISBN HARDBACK: 978-1-80566-723-0
ISBN PAPERBACK: 978-1-80566-852-7

Vital Currents

A root danced down with glee,
It thought it found a tree.
But tripped on worms along the way,
"Oops! Sorry!" it had to say.

The leaves above were busy clowns,
Poking fun from leafy crowns.
"Can you hear that?" one did shout,
"It's just that silly root, no doubt!"

The Whispering Ground

A beetle held a grand debate,
With ants about their lunch plate.
"What's better? Crumbs or leaves?" they jest,
As they squabbled over the best.

The dirt, quite tired of their row,
Muttered softly, "Oh, wow!
If I had hands, I'd close my ears,
To save myself from all your cheers."

Essence of the Horizon

A dandelion in the breeze,
Giggled at the passing cheese.
"Hey, look at that!" it sang with pride,
"I bet it wishes it could glide!"

A squirrel chuckled in delight,
As mushrooms danced in morning light.
"Oh what fun!" they all agreed,
"Life is silly, that's our creed!"

Unseen Threads of Life

A spider spun a story grand,
Of lost shoes and mismatched band.
"Hey, don't step there!" it cried in jest,
"A pebble's lurking, just like a pest!"

Beneath it worms have daily chats,
About silly hats and chubby rats.
"Why do we wiggle?" they all stare,
"Because wiggling's fun, that's fair!"

Roots of Memory

In the garden, I once found,
A carrot dancing on the ground.
It wiggled, jiggled, made a show,
Said, "You won't find friends down below!"

The turnips giggled, they took a stand,
"We're not just veggies, we're a band!"
With tiny hats and a sprout parade,
We laughed so hard, we nearly swayed!

Vitality in the Dark

In shadowed corners, things take flight,
A rogue potato claiming night!
He whispered tales of dirt and grime,
While radishes cracked jokes, oh so prime!

The squishy beet rolled in a spin,
"I've got my roots but love to grin!"
Laughter echoed through the pots,
Even mushrooms shared their thoughts!

Nectar from the Earth

The flowers brewed a potion sweet,
With buzzing bees that danced their feat.
"Try our cocktail, sip with glee!"
Cried daisies, "You'll feel so free!"

But daisies slipped, oh what a sight,
Lemonade in leafy light!
The blossoms laughed 'til dew was spilled,
A floral party, joy fulfilled!

Roots Beneath the Surface

Underneath, the chatter swells,
With onions swapping smelly spells.
"We're on a quest for fragrant fame!"
They dreamed of glory, oh what a game!

Carrots said, "Let's plant some cheer,
A comedy show, let's gather near!"
With roots entwined and spirits bright,
They shared their jokes, into the night!

Amber Rivers in the Dark

In shadows deep, a tale unfolds,
Of silly roots and secrets told.
The giggling buds, they tease and play,
While worms dance madly, come what may.

A squirrel with acorns on his head,
Claims he's the king of this leafy bed.
With twigs for swords, they fight with glee,
An unlikely band of tree-top tea.

Tapestry of Life's Breath

In the garden where laughter blooms,
Flowers wear hats, and dance in rooms.
The daisies gossip, the violets sing,
While carrots wear capes, just to be king.

Mice wear shoes suited for the lawn,
And jump like rabbits when pounced upon.
Each leaf a joke, each stem a pun,
Nature's humor, second to none.

Beneath the Quiet Canopy

Where the branches wiggle and sway,
A caterpillar raps in a funny way.
With a leafy beat, he croons at night,
'The trees are my fans; they cheer with delight!'

A fox in shades struts by with flair,
Claims he's the coolest critter out there.
While ants march on, with synchronized feet,
In a parade, oh so neat, yet sweet.

The Pulse of the Forgotten

In the shadows, roots create a scene,
A dance-off with toads, who thinks they're keen.
They twirl and leap, with warty flair,
While mushrooms giggle, filling the air.

A porcupine jokes, with quills in a twist,
'That backward tumble, oh, I can't resist!'
They all join in, the laughter grows wide,
In the heart of the earth, a joyful ride.

Harbingers of Green

Tiny sprouts emerge with glee,
Waving like they're at a spree.
With wholesome smiles, they stretch and sway,
Hoping sunshine won't go away.

Worms throw parties down below,
With roots as guests, they steal the show.
They chat of puddles and rainbows bright,
While ants do a conga, what a sight!

Subterranean Secrets

Down below, the chatter's wild,
Moles and beetles playing mild.
They tell tales of the moonlit night,
And snacks they've stashed, oh what a bite!

"Did you see that radish green?"
"It's bigger than a bear's hop scene!"
They giggle at the antics above,
As roots share gossip, truly a love.

Cradled in Earth's Arms

Nestled snug in nature's lap,
Buds and blooms fit for a nap.
They dream of rain and sunny cheer,
While ladybugs whisper, "Oh dear!"

A caterpillar starts to dance,
In rhythm with a dandelion's prance.
"Watch me twirl and spin this way,"
The flowers laugh, "What a display!"

The Unseen Supply

An underground crew works with flair,
Passing goodies everywhere.
With tiny hands, they hustle and scurry,
In the dark, there's no need to worry.

They stock up snacks for leafy friends,
With treats a-growing that never ends.
"We're the munchies' secret team,"
Laughing as they spread the cream!

The Fabric of Fertility

In the garden, a root takes a nap,
While talking to the worm in a hat.
They plot to grow a giant bean,
That'll make everyone laugh, it seems!

The carrots are dancing, waving hello,
While the radishes put on a show.
Potatoes whisper secrets of cheer,
As they peek from underground with no fear.

The rhythm of life, a constant tease,
With veggies becoming the best of buddies.
When summer fades and pumpkins bloom,
Everyone giggles, there's plenty of room!

So cherish the roots, so lively and spry,
As they plot and laugh beneath the sky.
Nature's comedy with every sprout,
Join the laughter; it's what it's about!

Nature's Ancestral Whisper

A tree told a joke to a passing breeze,
Which giggled and rustled through the leaves.
The flowers chuckled in vibrant hues,
Creating a symphony of nature's views.

Old rocks giggle at the tales they keep,
While moss shares secrets; they never sleep.
The breeze makes them dance, an ancient prank,
With laughter that echoes across the bank.

The rivers flirt with the banks so tight,
Splashing around with pure delight.
Each ripple carries a story or two,
A funny little tidbit for me and you.

In this wild world, the quips are loud,
As critters gather, so proud and endowed.
So lean in close, let nature play,
For the laughter of life is bright every day!

Hidden Oaths

Underneath the mushrooms, a pact is made,
Between the ants and the light that fades.
They swear to share crumbs and tasty treats,
While planning their parties on grassy seats.

The daisies with laughter hear the decree,
To throw a soirée down by the tree.
The thorns on the roses prick just a bit,
But their humor shines through, not a single split.

In the shadows, the chatter swells,
'Til beetles and bugs share their little spells.
All hidden oaths, wrapped in delight,
Lurking in laughter, they party all night.

Their whispers rise above the ground,
As beetles dance, and moss spins around.
In the heart of the earth, a camaraderie grows,
With each silly secret that only nature knows!

Life's Quiet Transfusion

A gentle breeze swirls by, oh what fun,
Tickling the blades of grass one by one.
The flowers giggle in splendid array,
While butterflies join in the playful ballet.

Squirrels are busy, with acorns to share,
Organizing a feast without a care.
They make little hats from the fallen leaves,
And dance in a circle, oh what a tease!

The sun winks down, a mischievous glow,
As shadows and colors play tag down below.
Each moment of laughter whispers around,
In this magical realm where joy knows no bounds.

So raise your glass, toast to the day,
For nature's humor is here to stay.
In the fabric of life, stitched snug and tight,
We all share a giggle in the soft twilight.

Elixirs of the Deep

In a goblet filled with greenish brew,
Worms dance jigs, oh what a view!
Mushrooms giggle, sprouting wide,
While beets wear capes, in roots they hide.

A gopher sips from a leafy cup,
Says it's magic, won't give up!
Carrots joke about their crunch,
As radishes punch their lunch!

The turnips think they've found the trick,
To grow a neck, all crops to pick!
Corn whispers tales of lost delight,
While peas throw parties every night.

So here's to potions, wild and free,
In the underground, such jubilee!
With laughter bubbling, oh what a cheer,
In the humor of the earth, we steer!

Secrets of the Warm Embrace

Cabbages gossip in the morning light,
About bugs that waltz, oh what a sight!
Beans wear hats, they stretch and spin,
While carrots play tag, let the games begin!

A potato boasts of its underground fame,
Says it's the center of every game!
Radishes laugh and sing for fun,
Their tops are the show, bright like the sun!

The onions shed tears, but it's all a jest,
Their layers of laughter, they love the fest.
Herbs strum tunes on vines, so fine,
As silly peppers dance in line!

Beneath the warmth, joy waves abound,
Life is a riot in this earthy ground.
With echoes of laughter all around,
In this embrace, who can frown?

Life's Hidden Veins

In the tunnels where the tiny critters meet,
They swap sweet tales, oh what a treat!
Nuts are the kings of this leafy land,
While mushrooms dispense their wisdom, so grand.

Grapes chuckle as they hang from a vine,
Sipping on sunshine, feeling divine!
Garlic whispers secrets, a pungent delight,
While squash plays peek-a-boo, such fun in sight!

The air is sprightly, with scents so sweet,
As veggies compose their own funny beat.
A drizzle of laughter, a sprinkle of cheer,
In the veins of the earth, joy's always near!

So here's to the harvest, wild and grand,
With every giggle that flows through the land.
In the dance of the roots, chaos reigns supreme,
Life's hidden veins are a whimsical dream!

Beneath the Canopy's Gaze

Under the arch of a leafy dome,
Squirrels chat wildly, making it home.
Berries throw parties, a colorful mess,
While blossoms don gowns, they're feeling their best!

Lettuce, the quiet one, rolls in the dirt,
Says it's just hiding, from all the exert.
Cucumbers giggle, they play peek-a-boo,
While radishes strut in their bright red hue!

The wind whispers jokes through the branches high,
As apples wink softly, no need to pry.
With laughter erupting from roots far below,
In the garden's embrace, joy starts to grow!

So raise a glass to the funny brigade,
Who thrive in the earth, in this sunny parade!
In the canopy's warmth, we laugh and we sway,
Life is a riot in leafy ballet!

Where Life Meets the Ground

In the garden, I lost my shoe,
A worm winked at me, what a view!
The daisies dance, in a funny way,
I laughed so hard, I might sway.

The carrots giggle underground,
Tickled by roots, oh what a sound!
Zucchini plays peek-a-boo with glee,
While peas pop out, to say, 'Look at me!'

The radishes crack jokes, oh so bright,
Under the sun, their humor's just right.
Butterflies flutter, trying to be cool,
Join the laughter, oh, what a school!

That garden's a riot, with joy in the air,
Where life meets the ground without a care.
Grab your hat and join the spree,
For the funniest show is for you and me.

The Beat of the Forest Floor

In the woods, where critters prance,
Squirrels do the cha-cha, oh what a chance!
The mushrooms giggle, beneath the trees,
Their caps all jiggling, swaying with ease.

A toad croaks out a croaky tune,
With frogs in the back, they dance 'til noon!
Rustling leaves join in the song,
As worms wiggle along, feeling strong.

Acorns roll with a playful thud,
While rabbits hop by in a funny flood.
A fox snickers at a slow old snail,
Who's lost in a race, without a trail!

The forest floor's a comedy show,
With creatures all laughing, putting on a glow.
Join in the fun, don't be a bore,
Where the beat of the wild is the best of lore.

Nourishing Shadows

In the shade, where shadows hide,
A gopher's got a joke, with pride.
The daisies gossip, whispering low,
About the sunflower's hairdo, quite the show!

A beetle's tap dance makes me grin,
While ladybugs cheer, "Let's begin!"
The tree trunks chuckle, swaying around,
As critters parade, without a sound.

The roots tickle, a secret delight,
While snails slide past, oh what a sight!
A shadowed party, a whimsical scene,
In this playful garden, all's evergreen.

So come take a seat, beneath leafy signs,
Where nourishing shadows weave funny lines.
Join the fun, let laughter unfold,
In the shadows of green, stories are told.

Echoes of Growth

In the garden where laughter expands,
Carrots tell tales with their leafy bands.
The broccoli chuckles in green, quite bright,
While tomatoes burst with giggles of light.

Pumpkins are rolling, making a fuss,
While squash serenades us, 'Won't you try us?'
The sprouts are a band, all eager to play,
As cucumbers whisper, 'It's a grand day!'

Sunshine drips laughter all through the air,
As busy bees buzz with naught a care.
Each seedling sprouts jokes, oh what a show,
With echoes of growth, they steal the glow!

A patch of fun, where nature will sing,
Where echoes of growth are the best of spring.
So laugh with the leaves and join the parade,
For this garden's a party, no joy will fade.

The Symphony of Growth

In the garden, a trumpet plays,
Radishes dance in their merry ways.
Carrots jiggle, peas leap high,
While spinach sings a lullaby.

A cucumber twirls in its green dress,
With each move, it causes a mess.
Zucchini joins in, but trips on a vine,
Laughing together, they all feel fine.

The beans bring some rhythm to the scene,
As broccoli twirls like a dancing queen.
A beetroot blushes, so shy and sweet,
While onions are crying with joy and defeat.

The night finally falls, the show's not done,
In the moonlight, the veggies still run.
Tomorrow they'll laugh and play once more,
In this wild garden where they all adore.

Forgotten Roots

Deep down below, where whispers grow,
A potato dreams of a lively show.
It recalls the days when it ruled the land,
Now covered and lost, it must make a stand.

The turnips gossip, "What's gone with Fred?"
He was last seen when they made their bed.
"Perhaps in soup, he'll grace a fine plate!"
"Or buried in butter, he'll surely be great!"

Radishes mock with their bright little smiles,
"Who needs to surface? We've got our styles!"
But deep in the dark, they dig and they scheme,
A root vegetable rebellion, it seems like a dream!

With laughter they plan, devising a plot,
To break free from earth, give it all they've got.
Together they'll rise, reclaiming their place,
As the kings of the garden, they'll win the race!

Silent Woods

In the woods where the critters creep,
A mushroom giggles, it won't lose sleep.
The trees tell jokes, but only at night,
While the flowers chuckle in morning light.

A squirrel in a tuxedo feels quite grand,
With acorn buttons, he takes his stand.
The ferns laugh hard, they can't hold it in,
As the critters gather for the dance to begin.

But wait—oh dear! A twig's fallen down,
The dance floor's rocked, it's a royal clown!
"Who stepped on my roots?" shouts the old oak tree,
"Watch where you leap, it's not about me!"

Yet all the creatures just roll on the ground,
Spreading the joy of the silliness found.
In silent woods, where laughter is bold,
Even the squirrels can't help but be sold!

Sunlight's Gentle Caress

A sunflower wakes with a yawn and a stretch,
Whispers to daisies, "You're looking fetch!"
The roses blush, with gossip they sway,
"Did you see Daisy? She's dressed for the day!"

The light drapes gold on the clover so green,
While daisies debate who is prettiest seen.
"Did you hear? The sun likes to play!"
Said one little bloom, "Join us on display!"

"There's no greater joy than the warmth on my face,
Let's dance and twirl, this is our place!"
The petals align in a colorful row,
At the whim of the light, they all start to flow.

But here comes the cloud with a frown and a pout,
"Oh dear, oh dear, there's a drought!"
Yet laughter prevails, with giggles they flower,
In the race of the sun, love's the true power!

The Life Beneath the Surface

In the dark of the earth, where secrets do hide,
A worm tells a tale, with great pride.
"We dig and we wriggle, we make quite a mess,
But in every garden, we bring success!"

"A beetle, oh beetle, we all need a chair!"
Said ant with a laugh, it's a tiny affair.
"Let's throw a party, under a radish leaf!"
Where all overhead, plot some truly rare grief.

The mole joins in with a top hat and flair,
"I'll flirt with the roots, they'll be in despair!"
Tunneling through, they snicker and tease,
In their little world, they do as they please.

But when morning dawns, and the sun's shining bright,
The critters above come out with delight.
While beneath them, a carnival of fun,
Worms whirl and twirl in the joy that they've spun!

Earthbound Echoes

In the dirt, the critters play,
Wiggling 'round both night and day.
A worm once wore a shiny hat,
Said, "I'm fabulous; how 'bout that?"

A beetle brags, his shell so bright,
Dances round, a funny sight.
He trips and falls upon a log,
Claims it's just a tricky frog.

With every root that tickles deep,
Earth's secrets sing, the laughter cheap.
A tiny ant sways in the breeze,
"I've got the moves, just watch me please!"

And yet a snail, he takes his time,
"Fast is cool, but slow's sublime!"
In this realm where giggles sprout,
The wise old tree just laughs about.

Murmurs of the Ancient

Underneath the old oak's shade,
Whispers dance in sunlight's glade.
A funny tale from roots of yore,
How gnomes lost keys to nature's door.

Acorns giggle, squirrels tease,
"Come play tag amongst the leaves!"
A sage old moss nods, wise and slow,
"Remember, kids, it's all for show!"

Through tangled vines, they weave their dreams,
While hidden mushrooms plot their schemes.
"Let's throw a party, what a thrill!"
Said the toadstool, "First, let's bake a quill!"

The wise old owl, perched up high,
Says funny things that make you sigh.
"Life's a laugh, just join the game,
Being earth-bound is never lame!"

The Cradle of Existence

In the cradle of the land so rich,
Where flowers bloom and bees do hitch.
A daisy jokes with prickle-thorn,
"Stop poking me! I feel so worn!"

A stout old cactus joins the fun,
"Just chill and bask in morning sun!"
The bumblebee buzzes with delight,
"Let's make this day a silly sight!"

The rocks chuckle, the stream will swirl,
As grass grows up to twirl and twirl.
What's the best way to laugh and dance?
Ask the dirt—a quirk-filled chance!

And as the sun dips low and sly,
The shadows stretch, the crickets cry.
"Make room for laughs!" the moonlight beams,
In this cradle, oddity gleams.

Whispers of the Underworld

Down below where shadows crawl,
Worms have parties, critters call.
Grubby fellows break out a tune,
While radishes moonwalk by the moon.

The gnome taps his root-bound shoes,
Sings of mets and earthworm blues.
"This dance floor's all the rage today,
Join in the fun—hurry, don't delay!"

Each pebble hums, a tinkle sound,
While mushroom caps bounce all around.
"Why so serious?" a mole will jest,
"Life's a game; come join the fest!"

As darkness wraps the world in cheer,
The laughs echo far, spreading near.
In the unseen, where laughter twirls,
The whispers of our earth give swirls.

The Pulse of the Undergrowth

In shadows where the critters play,
The wiggly roots dance night and day.
A tree once sneezed, oh what a scene,
Leaves fell down like confetti, so keen.

The beetles march in silly rows,
Shaking their tails in funny shows.
A worm had dreams of being a snake,
But tripped on roots, oh what a mistake!

The ants are busy, marching in time,
With tiny backpacks, oh so sublime.
Fungi giggle, wearing their caps,
In the land of worms and funny mishaps.

So wander deep where the laughter hums,
Join the party, see how it comes!
Digging here feels like a sport,
With every tiny giggle, we cavort.

Essence of the Deep

In the dark where mischief grows,
Bubbles pop like jokes, who knows?
A tiny fish slips on a scale,
While snails have their very own trail!

The playful frogs throw pondside bashes,
While the tadpoles giggle in funny splashes.
Grubs don sunglasses, strut with flair,
Playing the best hide-and-seek anywhere!

A kin of gnomes have a disco night,
With mushroom lamps that give off light.
Each step brings giggles from the ground,
As roots provide a boisterous sound.

So dive into the humor, so cheeky and bright,
Join the dance in the soft moonlight.
Every burble and bubble holds laughter's key,
Let's celebrate the joy where all critters be!

Life's Elixir

A drop of dew's a secret brew,
Sipping with bugs, an adventurous crew.
Ladybugs gossip, oh what a surprise,
While beetles share tales of their exercises!

Nature's potion, all ready to cheer,
The critters gather, spreading good cheer.
A clumsy ant trips, slipping on sweet,
And giggles erupt from tiny feet!

With blooms that giggle, petals that sway,
The sun brings a joke every lovely day.
Grass as a stage, where dance is the game,
Who knew that nature was never so tame?

So sip this laughter, from earth to sky,
Join the jesters, let out a sigh!
In our wild and wacky world, we'll unite,
For every drop's a laugh in the sunlight!

Earthen Embrace

With a hug from the ground, what a sight!
Each stone has a story, each root takes flight.
A squirrel with mittens dances on bows,
While worms play tag, and nobody knows!

The grass tickles toes, oh what a thrill,
While crickets throw parties, laughing at will.
The hedgehog dons shoes, oh what a sound,
As he rolls through the grass, round and round!

While the sun peeks out, like a giddy child,
The daisies get silly, all painted and wild.
Tiny little seeds gossip and giggle,
As the bumblebee trips in a busy wiggle.

So let's laugh with the land, feel the embrace,
Where the quirkiest creatures come out to race.
In every moment, a chuckle we find,
Join the fun, leave worries behind!

Cradle of Green

In a pot sits a plant so bold,
With secrets of ages, yet to be told.
It stretches and yawns, a grand leafy show,
"Water me, please! I'm ready to grow!"

A worm passes by, all slimy and slick,
"Excuse me! Sir! You're making me sick!"
The flower chortles, its petals ablaze,
"Join in my dance, let's end the malaise!"

Breath of the Wilderness

A squirrel in a tree, with acorns galore,
Hides them with glee, then forgets where they store.
"Now where did I put that tasty snack?"
"Ah well, no regrets, let's just eat this pack!"

The breeze whistles tunes as it tickles the leaves,
"Breathe out all your worries, for nature believes!"
Moss giggles softly, in shadows it lurks,
"We're just having fun, don't be such a jerk!"

Organic Ties

A beet and a carrot, best buddies they say,
"Let's make a salad, and party all day!"
They're tossed in a bowl with greens all around,
"What a fine mix, we're truly renowned!"

The herbs swoon and twirl, quite dizzy with cheer,
"Together we're magic, that much is clear!"
But then a cucumber slyly intrudes,
"Hold up, my friends, I've got the best moods!"

The Heart of the Forest

In the woods where the mischief-makers rule,
A fox with a hat makes quite the fool.
"I'll dance with the trees to my favorite beat!"
"Who needs a party? I bring the heat!"

The mushrooms chuckle, their caps in a spin,
"Let's boogie and jiggle, let the fun begin!"
A raccoon joins in, with a moonlit grin,
"With friends like this, we all always win!"

Foundations of Vitality

In a world of roots and clumps,
The tubers dream of sugar lumps.
They wiggle deep and have a chat,
'Who's got the best compost, and where's it at?'

Worms parade in festive lines,
Rocking out to dancing vines.
Giggling as they twist and twine,
Underneath the leafy shrine.

The earthworm's wiggle is a sight,
As veggies chuckle in delight.
Potatoes whisper 'We've got flair',
While carrots boast of health affair.

With each growl of hunger's call,
The peas and beans have quite a brawl.
They squabble over who's the best,
In this garden, a leafy fest!

Nature's Lifeblood

In the stillness of a sunny day,
The radishes are here to play.
They bounce around in rhythmic cheer,
While cucumbers smirk, 'We rule the year!'

A beet decides to throw a dance,
With greens all swaying in a trance.
Tomatoes laugh with juicy glee,
'You can't squish us; just wait and see!'

A ladybug rolls by with flair,
To judge who's got the finest hair.
The sunflowers turn and grin so wide,
While peas hide giggles deep inside.

As rain clouds gather, petals shout,
'We're having fun! Let's skip the doubt!'
They twirl and whirl, with joy, they clap,
In this green wonder, they take a nap!

Threads of Sustenance

In the garden's lively show,
The veggies strike a witty tableau.
Leeks blow bubbles in a row,
While radish roots steal the show.

A pumpkin wears a funny hat,
As onions laugh, 'Look at that!'
The garlic claps with zeal and zest,
In this little patch, they are the best!

Cabbages gossip in tight formation,
Whispering tales of sprout vacations.
Meanwhile, beets plan a wild race,
With carrots, who can't keep pace.

With laughter echoing through the leaves,
The herbs chime in, 'We're the thieves!'
For nature's jesters, bold and spry,
Create a scene that makes us sigh!

The Language of the Earth

Underneath the earth's warm glow,
The roots convey what we don't know.
They share their tales of twists and bends,
Through laughter that the soil sends.

A daisy pops up to recite,
'Knock, knock, who's there?'—'Not a fright!'
The carrots chuckle, 'What a jest!'
As beans declare, 'We're simply blessed!'

The fungi groove with funky flair,
Making friendships beyond compare.
They take a bow, then growl and shout,
'Let's have some fun; that's what it's about!'

In dirt they play their little game,
With laughter rising, never lame.
A joyous dance among the roots,
In nature's choir, who needs suits?

Sheltered Promises

In the garden, dreams collide,
With a sloth that's never tried.
A snail races, what a sight!
While I sip tea, feeling light.

Gnomes in hats, they wave hello,
Counting worms that steal the show.
Moles dig tunnels, quite the fuss,
"Excuse me, sir!" says a ladybus.

The daisies giggle, petals twirl,
A sprinkle of rain makes them whirl.
"Why so heavy?" the daisies tease,
"Just a drop!" says the breeze with ease.

In this patch of playful cheer,
A frog croaks gossip, loud and clear.
Chasing shadows, dancing cows,
Nature's jest, I take a bow!

The Cycle of Renewal

Every spring, the worms declare,
Tiny parties, everywhere!
Ants parade with tiny hats,
Crickets chirp—how about that?

The trees are sprouting, looking keen,
Blossoms blush in shades of green.
"Excuse my roots!" a flower shouts,
As dandelions toss about.

A ladybug, with charm so ripe,
Flirts with bees, a curious type.
Nature giggles, life's in tune,
While rabbits hop beneath the moon.

Who knew mud could be such fun?
Rolling in it when the day is done.
Nature's laugh, a silly sound,
In this world where joy is found!

Blood of the Battlefield

The ants, they march, a tiny crew,
In search of crumbs, what will they do?
With crumbs of bread, they build their throne,
"Glory to our crunchy cone!"

A caterpillar, in a trance,
Practices its wiggle dance.
"Hold my leaves!" it seems to shout,
While ladybugs just twirl about.

The grasshoppers sing in a band,
While earthworms cheer from the sand.
"Life's a party!" the crickets say,
As bees pollinate the fray.

In the garden wars, no one's mean,
Just mud-slinging, all in green.
Victory! A leaf's proud call,
For caterpillars, after all!

Beneath the Weight of Time

Underneath the leafy veil,
A tale told by a wrinkled snail.
"Time's too fast!" it seems to groan,
While daisies hum a little tone.

A worm whispers, "Have no fear,
Just wiggle on, and persevere!"
Each morning brings a brand-new day,
As flowers stretch and gently sway.

The oak tree's wisdom fills the air,
With acorns dropping, just beware!
Squirrels giggle, chasing tails,
While busy ants plot tiny trails.

So here we are, a funny rhyme,
A joyful dance through tricks of time.
Nature's punchline, bright and clear,
In this green world, we laugh and cheer!

The Underground Symphony

In tunnels dark, the whispers play,
Worms do dance, in a strange ballet.
Fungi giggle, in their own tune,
Mushrooms juggling beneath the moon.

Beneath the ground, the roots take flight,
Tickling each other, oh what a sight!
The beetles tap their little toes,
While ants march on, wearing fine clothes.

Critters munch on organic treats,
Crafting banquets from leftover beats.
"Oh dear worm, is that a snack?"
"Only if it's not from my pack!"

Life goes on in this lively pit,
With laughter and snacks, they never quit.
So next time you walk on that ground,
Remember the party where joy's unbound.

Tapestry of Life

In layers deep, the world does weave,
Nature giggles, oh can you believe?
With each tiny sprout, a story's spun,
Tales of broccoli having fun.

Carrots wearing capes, what a sight!
Dancing radishes, filled with delight.
"Join us!" shouts the parsnip, so bright,
"Together we'll party into the night!"

Roots entwined like best friends, they say,
Sharing secrets in a humorous way.
"Oh, I once tripped over that stone!"
"Not again!" yells the potato, well-known.

They all share a laugh, a hearty hoot,
Over the mischief some creatures loot.
So when you taste that salad so fine,
Remember the fun that's all intertwined.

Woven Threads of Nature

In the garden, laughter thrives,
Where each little sprout truly survives.
The beans tease the peas with a grin,
"Watch me climb, let the fun begin!"

Under the surface, the giggles grow,
With root races that put on a show.
"Catch me if you can!" shouts a sly seed,
While tangled up in their playful deed.

Beetles play tag, such crafty spies,
While earthworms laugh with their squiggly lies.
The daisies roll on the floor in glee,
As flowers bloom in harmony.

So when you see flora, don't just admire,
Join in the jest, dance by the fire.
For within the earth, where the fun is found,
Laughter and life are beautifully bound.

Currents of Growth

Oh, what a riot beneath our feet,
As roots shimmy and worms skip a beat.
"Let's race!" shouts the sprout with a cheer,
While a crabapple winks, "I've got nothing to fear!"

Plants gossip sweet, with a giggling breeze,
"Did you hear what the nettlet said with ease?"
"Let's sprout a rumor, just for fun!"
And giant zinnias blush in the sun.

Life's a dance in this underground sphere,
Where leaves whisper secrets we all hold dear.
"Where's the party?" asks a clover with zest,
"Right here!" yells the dandelion, "It's the best!"

So, when you wander in nature's show,
Remember the joy that keeps it aglow.
For every giggle and tiny jest,
Is a celebration that nature knows best.

The Dark Kiss of Life

In a coffee cup, a garden grows,
With little beans and tiny toes.
Laughing leaves dance in the breeze,
Winking roots whisper with ease.

A worm in a tux, what a sight!
Proposing to a plant, in the moonlight.
They tango and twirl, oh what a show,
Do you dare to join? Give it a go!

Rain does a jig, stomping on roofs,
While flowers gossip in silly hooves.
Bees wearing shades on their buzzing spree,
Winking at blooms like they own the spree.

The sun plays peek-a-boo with the day,
As branches chuckle in their own way.
So raise your cup, toast life in disguise,
For chaos in nature is quite the prize!

Beneath the Bark and Bone

Under the crust, there's laughter so deep,
Where earthworms plot and tree roots creep.
A squirrel in shorts, with shades on his eyes,
Declares nutty parties—a nutty surprise!

Fungi in hats are hosting their prom,
With mossy green carpets, they dance till dawn.
Toadstools groove in the moon's soft glow,
Even beetles join in, putting on a show!

A grumbling brook hums a tune so slick,
While pebbles chuckle, doing a little trick.
Grass blades whisper jokes, tickling the toes,
Of busy ants debating which way to go.

So next time you walk past that shady tree,
Remember the parties, oh jubilee!
For life's a big circus, never too grim,
With each little creature, life starts to brim!

Wellspring of Existence

Down in the depths, where the giggles flow,
Potatoes plot trips to the farmer's show.
Carrots in sunglasses soak up the sun,
Comedians of dirt, oh what fun!

A rubbery plant tried to do a stunt,
But tripped on a bug, what a clumsy hunt!
Cabbages chuckled, rolling in glee,
At every twist of this earthy spree.

Desserts made of dirt, oh the flavor sublime,
Chocolate mud pies that are so hard to mime.
"Let's eat the garden!" cries a brave bee,
While the daisies giggle, "Not if you ask me!"

So sip on some dew, take a moment to cheer,
For earth's silly shenanigans, oh my dear!
In the well of existence, joy does abound,
Where laughter's the nectar in every sound!

Ties to the Living Past

Old roots tell tales of days gone by,
Of cozy bugs and birds who fly.
A time traveler rose with a curly plant,
Waving to flowers, the best little chant!

The grand oak tree wears a historical crown,
Whispering secrets without a frown.
While ladybugs sketch in the green on the side,
Drawing the laughter that life can't hide.

Beneath each leaf, a story's untold,
Of seedlings with dreams that are ever so bold.
The past tickles roots, it's all a big jest,
In the playground of nature, we're all just guests!

So twirl around the grass, feel history's sway,
With each little sprout, celebrate today!
For life's a connection—a humorous flight,
In the dance of the living, everything's bright!

Sinews of Creation

In the garden, things get funny,
Worms laugh at seeds, oh, so runny.
Pests wear glasses, think they're slick,
While lettuce folks do a dance, quick!

The radish says, 'I'm on a roll!'
While carrots pull with all their soul.
Beets try to boast, a crimson shout,
But gophers giggle and run about!

Sunflowers glance, and wink a bit,
As bees buzz by, giving a hit.
"Oh what a day!" they all exclaim,
Nature's wackiness is their game!

With roots and sprouts, the jokes abound,
Life underground is quite the sound.
A tickle, a chuckle, a laugh so spry,
In this wild place, everyone's high!

From Darkness Comes Light

In the pitch-black night, a sprout takes flight,
Says, 'I'll shine bright, like a disco light!'
Turtles chuckle, 'What's that you say?'
A glowworm replied, 'I'm here to stay!'

The mushrooms dance, a wobble and sway,
'Join us, dear friend, let's party today!'
But a nearby bush just snickers and leans,
'You fungi folk, just look at your jeans!'

A firefly winks, a clever delight,
'I was voted best-dressed on this starry night!'
Crickets are tuning their bands for a show,
While the moon rolls her eyes, 'Oh, stop with the glow!'

Yet through all the giggles, a truth lies below,
With laughter and light, the best friendships grow.
It's a whimsical dance, earth's own little sight,
From the dark comes the fun, oh what a delight!

Hidden Waters in the Wild

Behind thick brush, mischief brews,
A frog croaks tunes while the duck snooze.
The river giggles 'neath leafy hats,
While fish tease turtles and dance like brats!

A splash here, a splash there, oh what a sight,
Toads and newts sing songs of delight.
Old raccoon, wise, with a grin so sly,
Says, 'Under the bridge, there's a pie in the sky!'

The dragonfly twirls, a dance so chic,
'Catch me if you can, you slowpoke freak!'
While minnows bootlegged moonlit beer,
To toast the night and not shed a tear.

With ripples and laughter, the waters gleam,
In this hidden nook, it's all a dream.
The wild knows how to tickle the pink,
Nature's jesters never cease to blink.

The Breath of the Canopy

Above the world, in a leafy realm,
The birds are giggling, at the helm.
'What's the rush?' asks the old wise tree,
'Life's just a game, come hang out with me!'

Squirrels chuckles as they leap and glide,
While raccoons scold from the branch side.
'There's a party up-high,' the willow sways,
'Trees tell tales of their juicy days!'

The breeze whispers secrets, ticklish and grand,
While clouds throw shade, like a fun band.
Laughter floats on the summer air,
Nature's fest is beyond compare!

So raise a toast with the acorns around,
In the heart of the woods, joy is found.
With each rustle, a chuckle anew,
In the canopy's breath, there's always a view!

Unraveling Nature's Logic

In the garden, plants do chat,
With laughter that makes the earth go 'pat'.
A sunflower winks at a nearby bean,
While the carrots giggle, oh what a scene!

The roots are tickled, they squirm and dive,
As the worms throw a party, oh, how they thrive!
The daisies dance in a breezy sway,
While the moles play hide-and-seek all day!

With each raindrop, jokes start to flow,
The violets are snickering, "Listen, you know?"
The trees shake hands, or is that a wave?
Nature's humor? It's quite the rave!

So here's to the green with a chuckle and cheer,
Their jokes so tall, let's lend them an ear!
In this quirky realm, life's a playful play,
Let's soak up the giggles, come what may!

Dance of Elements Below

Down in the dark where the fun never stops,
The fungi are hosting the wildest hops!
The roots can't help but boogie around,
Where the microbes are kings, let's gather 'round!

The pH scale's snickering in a twist,
While nutrients shout, "Don't let us be missed!"
With calcium here and oxygen too,
They all share a chuckle, a merry hullabaloo!

Little critters bustle and skitter and skedaddle,
With tiny beetles leading the grand new raddle.
Sprouting laughter from the underground den,
Nature's funniest crew, again and again!

So come take a dip in this loamy delight,
Where every root wiggles with joyful insight.
Down in the dirt, life's a whimsical game,
Whispers of humor, but who's really to blame?

Cradle Songs of the Hidden

In a cozy nook where the shadows play,
The seedlings hum sweet tunes at the end of the day.
The peas sing softly to the sleeping beans,
While the gophers join in, in their leafy scenes!

With lullabies drifting through every leaf,
The broccoli croons, but don't ask for belief.
A chorus of herbs, so fragrant and bright,
They weave the night songs till the morning light!

The beetroot's voice, it's low and round,
While the radish dances without making a sound.
Together they form a band, oh so sly,
With nature's quirks, they reach for the sky!

So close your eyes, let their laughter ring,
Under the stars, every plant has a fling.
As they sway to the rhythm of crickets' delight,
Nature's cradle songs and the joy they excite!

Secrets of Botanical Kinship

Once upon a twig, there's a tale to unfold,
Of plants that gossip, a band, brave and bold.
The daisies decree, "We're the flower elite!"
While cacti spin yarns of desert retreat!

The mushrooms join in, with a wink and a grin,
"Watch us grow stories from within!"
The tulips all tease with colors so grand,
Making lovely friendship bands in the sand!

Whispers of roots, all tangled and sly,
Plotting to send the ants on a high.
Together they giggle, a botanical scheme,
Sharing secrets beneath one big leafy dream!

With petals aflutter and joy all around,
In this lively garden, good vibes abound.
So let's tip our hats to this green jubilee,
Where kinship is bonded in a leafy spree!

www.ingramcontent.com/pod-product-compliance
Lightning Source LLC
Chambersburg PA
CBHW072137200426
43209CB00050B/69